Date August 25/04

Dear
Coreen,
    I hope this book will encourage you through this time. Praying for you and Ryan.

From
Kara

You're in my Prayers

Art and text © Karla Dornacher, licensed by Suzanne Cruise
Artwork and text licensed by J Countryman, used by permission.

© 2003 Christian Art Gifts, RSA
         Christian Art Gifts Inc., IL, USA

Designed by Christian Art Gifts

Unless otherwise indicated, Scripture is taken from the *Holy Bible*, New International Version®. NIV®. Copyright © 1973, 1978, 1984 by International Bible Society. Used by permission of Zondervan Publishing House. All rights reserved.

Scripture quotations marked NLT are taken from the *Holy Bible*, New Living Translation, copyright © 1996. Used by permission of Tyndale House Publishers, Inc., Wheaton, Illinois 60189. All rights reserved.

Scripture quotations marked KJV taken from the *Holy Bible*, King James Version. Copyright © 1962 by The Zondervan Corporation. Used by permission.

Scripture quotations marked NKJV taken from the *Holy Bible*, New King James Version. Copyright © 1979, 1980, 1982 by Thomas Nelson Publishers, Inc. Used by permission. All rights reserved.

Printed in China

ISBN 1-86920-329-1

03   04   05   06   07   08   09   10   11   12   –   10   9   8   7   6   5   4   3   2   1

You're
in my
Prayers

KARLA DORNACHER

christian
art gifts

We do not cease
to pray for you, and
ask ... that you may
walk worthy of the
Lord, fully pleasing
Him, being fruitful
in every good work
and increasing in the
knowledge of God.

Colossians 1:9~10, NKJV

Enter His gates
with thanksgiving

welcome

Psalm 100:4

God is calling your name,
inviting you to come into His presence
and enjoy His company.
I pray for you today my friend
that during your time alone with God,
you will enter His presence
with praise and thanksgiving.
I pray that before you even begin
to tell Him your needs,
wants and desires,
that you will take a moment
to tell Him how incredibly wonderful
He is and how grateful you are
for all He has already done in your life.

In everything, by prayer and petition,
with thanksgiving,
present your requests to God.

Philippians 4:6

7

The fruit of the Spirit is
love, joy, peace, patience,
kindness, goodness, faithfulness,
gentleness, and self~control.

Galatians 5:22~23

♥

And this is my prayer: that your
love may abound more and more
in knowledge and depth of insight,
so that you may be able to discern
what is best and may be pure and
blameless until the day of Christ,
filled with the fruit of righteousness
that comes through Jesus Christ ~
to the glory and praise of God.

Philippians 1:9~11

Dear Lord,

Fill my friend with the
wonderful, fragrant, fruitful
brew of Your Holy Spirit.

Fill her so full Lord,
that the fruit of the Spirit
will pour out of her heart
and bless the people
You've placed along her path
with a refreshing drink of You.

Let the fruit of her lips
praise You,
and the fruit of her life
bring You glory.

Bless her with great fruitfulness.

In Christ's Name ... Amen.

9

You are His
workmanship
Ephesians 2:10

Father God,

Thank You for my friend!
She is such an incredible blessing in my life.

Lord, I am so glad that You made her just the way
You did...right down to the number of hairs on
her head...and the color of them too! I'm so glad
You knit her together in her mother's womb
and created her in Your image and for Your glory.
She truly is fearfully and wonderfully made ~
one of a kind by Your creative design.

Father, I pray for my friend today
that You will always enable her to see herself
through Your loving eyes ~
not her own or the world's.
Remind her how there is only one of her
and only she can fulfill that perfect plan
that You have designed especially for her.

Bless her today with confidence
in who You've made her to be.

In Christ's Name...Amen.

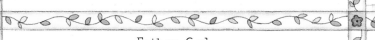

Father God,

I pray that, by Your Spirit,
You will enable my friend to know,
more and more every day ~
how long, how wide, how deep and how high
Your love for her truly is ~
and that, no matter where she is
or what she is going through,
nothing can separate her from
Your unconditional, overwhelming love.

Bless her with Your presence.

In Jesus' Name … Amen.

"Be strong and of good courage; do not be
afraid, nor be dismayed, for the LORD
your God is with you wherever you go."

Joshua 1:9

My dear friend,

God's Word promises that when we pray ~
whether it is for a loved one to know Jesus,
the means to pay next month's bills, or any
other need or heart's desire ~ He truly does
hear our prayers and is faithful to answer.
I pray that you will know, without a doubt,
that God's promises are true.
He has heard your prayers
and is already at work on your behalf.
I pray as you wait on Him for the answer,
that He will increase your faith
and guard your heart from unbelief.

Lord, help my friend to stay focused on You
and the promises of Your Word.
Bless her with patient endurance.

In Christ's Name ... Amen.

Your promises are
sweet to me,
sweeter than honey in my mouth!

My dear friend,

I pray for you today
that in the midst of the trials and
tribulations you are going through,
you will draw near to God
and find comfort and rest in His arms.
I pray also . . . that a heart of thanksgiving
will be your strength
as you remember
God's blessings in the good times,
His faithfulness in the hard times,
and His love at all times.

In everything give thanks; for this
is the will of God in Christ Jesus for you.
1 Thessalonians 5:18, NKJV

Dear Lord,
I am so thankful
for my friend.
I ask that you
would strengthen
her today with your
love and give her
direction and guidance
according to your
promises. Amen

Dear Jesus,
You are the best
friend a girl could
ever hope for

Love shared warms the heart

And hope does not disappoint us,
because God has poured out His love
into our hearts by the Holy Spirit,
whom He has given us.

Romans 5:5

Father God,

Thank You
for pouring out a drink
of Your tender love
to warm the heart
of my dear friend.
I pray for her today Lord,
that she will receive
every drop of blessing
You have for her
so that her cup
is not only full,
but that it spills over
into the lives of those
You've placed along her path.

Bless her today
with a heart overflowing.

In Christ's Name … Amen.

19

For we are God's workmanship,
created in Christ Jesus to do good works,
which God prepared in advance for us to do.
Ephesians 2:10

Father,

You are the Potter and Your
handiwork is incredible.
It fascinates me how You could create
each of us so unique and individual.

I pray for my friend today,
that You will enable her to accept
and embrace her own uniqueness
in every aspect of her life.
Give her eyes to see that she
is Your vessel, filled with the
treasure of Your sweet Spirit.
Help her discover the gifts, talents,
and abilities You've given her
so that she may know the joy
of being tipped over for Your glory
and the blessing of many.

Bless her to fulfill all
You've designed her to be.

In Christ's Name … Amen.

21

My dear friend,

No one is exempt from times of trouble ~ not one of us. And so I pray, as you face the storms of life, that you will always know that Jesus calls you to come away with Him and find shelter and safety in the pavilion of His tender care.

I pray that His pavilion will be to you a hiding place ~ a safe haven ~ where you will be able to be still in His presence, hear His voice, taste His goodness, worship His holiness, and trust Him as your best Friend.

Bless my friend with Your Presence, Lord.

In Jesus' Name ... Amen.

But let all who take refuge in You rejoice; let them sing joyful praises forever. Protect them, so all who love Your name may be filled with joy.

Psalm 5:11, NLT

In the time of trouble He shall hide me in His Pavilion.

Psalm 27:5

Welcome

Worship — Praising God because He is worthy

Submission — Desiring God's will and not your own

Petition — Praying for your own needs

Intercession — Praying for the needs of others

Forgiveness — Seeking God's forgiveness for yourself / Forgiving those who have hurt or offended you

Thanksgiving — Thanking God for all He does and who He is

Dear Heavenly Father,

I worship and adore You and thank You
for giving me this special friend.
I pray for her today and ask
for Your perfect will in her life.
I pray You meet all of her needs.
Bless her family and friends, Lord.
Forgive her of her sins and
enable her to forgive the sins of others.
Fill her heart with thanksgiving
as she considers all You are and
all You have done on her behalf.

Bless her with the fragrance of Christ.

In Jesus' Holy Name ... Amen.

We are
to God
the fragrance
of Christ

I will trust in the shelter of your wings

I will trust in the shelter of your wings

I will trust in the shelter of your wings

I will trust in the shelter of your wings

God has promised
to be your hiding place,
your refuge
when you seek protection,
and a safe haven
when you need to retreat.

Under the shadow of His wings
nothing can harm you.

AMAZING GRACE,
HOW SWEET
THE
SOUND

I pray for you
to see God's glory,
behold the beauty
of His face,
to hear His voice
and walk in the joy
of His awesome,
amazing grace.

And the Word became flesh
and dwelt among us,
and we beheld His glory,
the glory as of the only begotten
of the Father,
full of grace and truth.

John 1:14, NKJV

I pray for you today my friend,
in this world of fear and stress,
that you will make a conscious choice
in the midst of your busyness ~

To set aside time alone,
to seek and pursue God's best,
so He can fill your heart and mind
with peace and give you rest.

Return to your rest, O my soul,
for the LORD has dealt bountifully with you.

Psalm 116:7, NKJV

My dear friend,

My heart cries out for you.
I know that you are hurting
and need more than I am able to give.
God said that He is near to the brokenhearted
and He is near to you even now.
I pray that you will sense His presence
and know that His arms are wrapped around
you with intense love and compassion.

Father God,

Comfort and encourage my friend
as only You can. Help her to know
that You are near. Bless her with Your
ever~present spirit of hope and comfort.

In Jesus' Name ... Amen.

Praise be to the God and Father
of our Lord Jesus Christ, the Father of
compassion and the God of all comfort,
who comforts us in all our troubles.

2 Corinthians 1:3~4

A day
hemmed
in prayer
seldom
unravels

I pray that you might know God
more and more every day.
I pray that you would know Him
in a close and intimate way.

Because the more you know God,
the more in love you'll grow.
The more you love and trust Him,
the more joy you will know.

For He alone is the one true God,
besides Him there's no other.
Only He can fill your heart
so you'll never seek another.

Be still and know that I am God.

Psalm 46:10

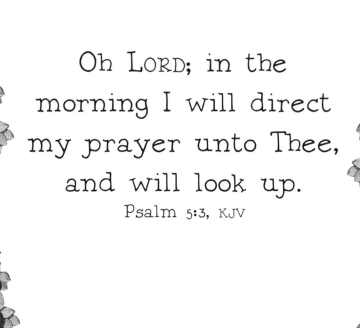

Oh LORD; in the morning I will direct my prayer unto Thee, and will look up.

Psalm 5:3, KJV

The Lord bless you and keep you; the Lord make His face shine upon you . . .

Numbers 6:24,25

40

Dear Jesus,

I pray for the joy of the Lord to overtake my friend as she considers the truth that Your face truly does shine upon her, Your smile envelops her, Your blessings go before her, and Your loving~kindness keeps her in Your care. In this place of incredible grace, may she delight herself in You as much as You delight in her.

Bless her with this truth.

In Christ's Name ... Amen.

Take delight in the LORD, and He will give you your heart's desire.
Psalm 37:4, NLT

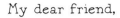

My dear friend,

I pray today
that God will open your eyes to see
the ordinary things of life
in extraordinary ways ~
the rising of the sun,
running water,
family blessings undeserved.

I pray wherever there has been
discontent in your heart,
that God will replace it
with an attitude of gratitude
and that
contentedness and thanksgiving
will be the trademark of your life.

Bless my friend, Lord.

In Jesus' Precious Name ... Amen.

I am the vine; you are the branches... abide in Me...

John 15:5
NKJV

44

Father God,

You truly are the vine and I thank You that my dear friend is one of Your beautiful branches. I'm glad that You love her so much and You see so much potential in her life that You have scheduled pruning times in her life to enable her to become more and more fruitful with every passing season.

I know pruning is not easy Lord, in fact, it can be quite painful and so I ask, as You cut away the dead or unfruitful branches in her, that You will imme~diately bind up the open wounds and bring swift healing so that even in the midst of the process of pruning, she will be blessed and You will be glorified in her life.

I ask this all in Jesus' Name ... Amen.

As the Spirit of the Lord works within us, we become more and more like Him and reflect His glory even more.
2 Corinthians 3:18, NLT

Your soul shall be like a well~ watered garden.

Jeremiah 31:14

Dear Lord,

I thank You so much for my friend and how You have caused her to grow, blossom and bear fruit ~ even fruit that is hidden from her sight.

I pray for her today that You would pour out Your Living Water into her life and saturate any dry and barren places that need a special touch from You, Lord. Bring new and vibrant life to any dream or vision that has been lying dormant. Enable her to continue to grow and become the beautiful, bountiful, well~watered garden You designed her to be.

Bless her with Your glory.

In Jesus' Name ... Amen.